DEVOTIONS INSPIRED BY
BEYOND BLESSED

Devotions Inspired by *Beyond Blessed*

Copyright © 2019 by Gateway Church

Written by *Robert Morris, James Morris, Jimmy Evans, Zach Neese, Chelsea Seaton, Mike Brisky, Phillip Hunter, Jelani Lewis, Tom Lane, Tim Ross, Preston Morrison, S. George Thomas, Thomas Miller, Allan Kelsey, Stacy Burnett, David Thompson, Mallory Bassham, Mary Jo Pierce, Mike Foltynski, Elizabeth Settle, Josh Morris*

Editorial Director *Shea Tellefsen*
Senior Editor *Daniel Hopkins*
Contributing Editor *Stacy Burnett*
Copy Editor *Georgette Shuler*
Project Coordinator *Liz Lowrie*

Creative Director *Justin Miller*
Art Director *Tim Lautensack*
Designer *Christy Kaneta*
Production Designer *Emanuel Puscas*
Print Coordinator *David Phillips*

Requests for information should be addressed to:
Gateway Publishing, 2250 E Continental Blvd, Suite 150, Southlake, TX 76092

Unless otherwise indicated, all Scripture is taken from the New King James Version®. Copyright © 1982 by Thomas Nelson. Used by permission. All rights reserved.

Scripture taken from the NEW AMERICAN STANDARD BIBLE®, Copyright © 1960, 1962, 1963, 1968, 1971, 1972, 1973, 1975, 1977, 1995 by The Lockman Foundation. Used by permission.

Scripture citations marked NIV are taken from *The Holy Bible, New International Version® NIV®* Copyright © 1973, 1978, 1984, 2011 by Biblica, Inc.® Used by permission. All rights reserved worldwide.

Scripture citations marked NLT are taken from the *Holy Bible, New Living Translation,* Copyright © 1996, 2004, 2015 by Tyndale House Foundation. Used by permission of Tyndale House Publishers, Inc., Carol Stream, Illinois 60188. All rights reserved.

The ESV® Bible (The Holy Bible, English Standard Version®). ESV® Text Edition: 2016. Copyright © 2001 by Crossway, a publishing ministry of Good News Publishers. The ESV® text has been reproduced in cooperation with and by permission of Good News Publishers. Unauthorized reproduction of this publication is prohibited. All rights reserved.

Scripture quotations marked TPT are from The Passion Translation®. Copyright © 2017, 2018 by Passion & Fire Ministries, Inc. Used by permission. All rights reserved. ThePassionTranslation.com.

Some names and details of actual events have been changed to protect the identities of the persons involved.

All rights reserved. No portion of this publication may be reproduced, stored in a retrieval system, or transmitted in any form by any means—electronic, mechanical, photocopying, recording, or any other— except for brief quotations in printed reviews, without the prior permission of the publisher.

Printed in the United States of America.

ISBN # 978-1-949399-44-8

CONTENTS

	Preface...7	
Day 01	**The Ownership Issue** *by Robert Morris*.................................. 11	
Day 02	**It Starts with Your Heart** *by James Morris*............................15	
Day 03	**Stewarding Your Spouse** *by Jimmy Evans*...............................19	
Day 04	**Parenting Like a Steward** *by Zach Neese*............................... 23	
Day 05	**Boom!** *by Chelsea Seaton* 27	
Day 06	**A Thoughtful Manager** *by Mike Brisky*....................................31	
Day 07	**Honor Your Family** *by Phillip Hunter*...................................... 35	
Day 08	**Head, Shoulders, Knees, and Toes** *by Jelani Lewis* 39	
Day 09	**You *Are* a Role Model** *by Tom Lane*... 43	
Day 10	**Jesus' Farming Advice** *by Tim Ross*.. 47	
Day 11	**The Stewardship of Submission** *by Jimmy Evans*................................51	

Day 12	**Who's the Boss?** *by Preston Morrison*	55
Day 13	**A Platform of Influence** *by S. George Thomas*	59
Day 14	**The Creative Invite** *by Thomas Miller*	63
Day 15	**God-Sized Invitations** *by Allan Kelsey*	67
Day 16	**Two Legs Required** *by Robert Morris*	71
Day 17	**Letting Go** *by Stacy Burnett*	75
Day 18	**Have You Been Faithful?** *by James Morris*	79
Day 19	**Talents and Spiritual Gifts** *by David Thompson*	83
Day 20	**The Most Important Thing** *by Mallory Bassham*	87
Day 21	**Reframe Your Day** *by Mary Jo Pierce*	91
Day 22	**I Give Up** *by Mike Foltynski*	95
Day 23	**Redeem the Earth** *by Josh Morris*	99
Day 24	**Take Care of Your Temple** *by Robert Morris*	103
Day 25	**Dashboard Lights** *by Elizabeth Settle*	107
Day 26	**The Order of Love** *by Jimmy Evans*	111
Day 27	**Stewarding a Miracle** *by Jimmy Evans*	115
Day 28	**The Principle of Rest** *by Robert Morris*	119
	Memory Verses	*123*

PREFACE

I'm so glad you're reading this devotional! The 28 devotions included were all inspired by my new book, *Beyond Blessed: God's Perfect Plan to Overcome All Financial Stress*, which is actually a sequel—or more like a prequel—to *The Blessed Life*. When I released *The Blessed Life* almost 20 years ago, it motivated the body of Christ around the world to live out the biblical truth of generosity and begin giving extravagantly. I named it *The Blessed Life*, not *The Blessed Pocketbook* or *The Blessed Wallet*, because when God changes a person's heart from selfishness to generosity, every part of their life is affected, not just their finances.

I have a tremendous burden for people to understand that living the blessed life is not only about being generous, it's also about stewardship. Merriam-Webster defines stewardship as, "The careful and responsible management of something entrusted to one's care." As believers, we recognize everything we have has been given to us by God. This includes money, but it also means our families, relationships, and health—even our own bodies. As we will discover in the 28 days that make up this devotional, all these things have been entrusted to us by God, and it's our job to steward them carefully and responsibly.

Because God has entrusted many things to us, you may start to feel like you have too many things to manage. However, if you rely on God, *He* will give you the grace to become a wise and faithful steward, which in turn, will ultimately lead to more freedom and margin in your life. Think of it like a budget. It might feel confining and restricting at first, but in the end, it helps us enjoy life more. In the same way, understanding the biblical principles of stewardship changes *everything* and helps us focus on what's really important—our relationship with God, family, and others.

At the conclusion of each devotion, we end with the question, "What is the Holy Spirit saying to me?" I want to encourage you to ask yourself this question every day because I believe God wants to speak to you through it. I promise that if you do this and allow God to show you how you can be the best steward of all He's given you, blessings will pour into your life and you can start living *beyond blessed*.

Pastor Robert Morris

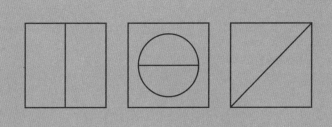

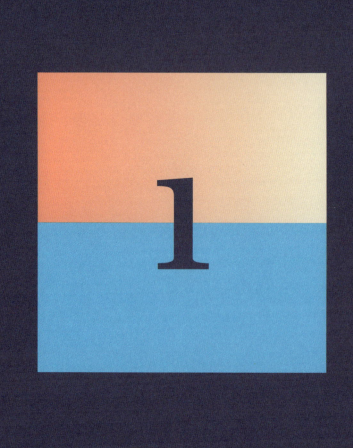

Day 1 | *by Robert Morris*
THE OWNERSHIP ISSUE

The earth is the Lord's, and everything in it. The world and all its people belong to him. Psalm 24:1 (NLT)

Have you ever seen two toddlers fighting over a toy? If you have, you know exactly how it works. Each one holds onto the toy tightly as they both shout "Mine!" With three children and now nine grandchildren, I've seen this scenario play out many times. Ironically, many times the toy they're fighting over doesn't even belong to them. It belongs to someone else. With our family, it was usually a toy Debbie or I bought for them.

How many times do we look at the "toys" we have and think *"Mine!"*? Maybe it's a house, car, job, relationship, or even money. The truth is, everything on earth is God's. Just look at today's verse, Psalm 24:1. Everything in our possession came from Him. Even our lives. This leads me to a deeper question: To whom do you belong?

If you have given your life to Jesus, it's an easy answer. You belong to God! While it may seem simple, this is one of the fundamental issues that shapes our lives as Christians, because when we realize our lives actually belong to God, we start acting differently. The same thing happens when we realize our stuff really isn't "our stuff." It doesn't belong to us, it belongs to God.

When you borrow something valuable from a friend—say, a car—you're more likely to drive a little more carefully and return it in better condition than you received it. How much would change if you acted this way with everything you have, including your life? It's one of the most important things to consider in our Christian lives, because until we settle the question of ownership in our hearts, we cannot truly be good stewards. In fact, recognizing that everything belongs to God is where stewardship begins in our lives. You'll be amazed at the changes that take place in your life when you adopt this mindset.

As you read through this devotional over the next 28 days, I encourage you to do so with this truth in mind: *everything I have belongs to God, including my life*. Once you change your thinking on this issue (and your actions follow accordingly), you'll begin to see that you belong to a generous God who wants to give you more blessings and gifts than you can imagine.

PRAYER

Lord, thank You for trusting me to be a steward of everything you've put in my care. I choose to believe that everything belongs to You, and I pray that You will show me how and give me the grace to become a better steward. In Jesus' name, Amen.

> **WHAT IS THE HOLY SPIRIT SAYING TO ME?**

FOR FURTHER STUDY
1 Corinthians 6:19–20; Psalm 50:10–12

Day 2 | *by James Morris*
IT STARTS WITH YOUR HEART
■●▲

"... for one's life does not consist in the abundance of the things he possesses." Luke 12:15

At Gateway we have a car donation ministry where people donate vehicles that we give to members in need. All kinds of cars have been donated. I've seen cars you might find in a junk yard, very nice new cars, and everything in between. For years I had the privilege to oversee this ministry, and in doing so I drove many of these vehicles. I would drive a car to the shop when repairs were needed and the car wash to clean it up right before we gave it to a member—whatever was necessary.

One day I drove a fully loaded 2-year-old BMW 7 series that was donated. It had dark windows and shiny wheels, and I got many comments when I drove it, and those comments made me feel good even though the car wasn't mine. On another day, I was driving an old, beat up Buick that was putting off some intense fumes. God used that Buick to teach me a valuable lesson.

I was driving through a nice town and hadn't eaten lunch that day. I pulled into a Chick-fil-A drive-through forgetting the windows didn't go down and the driver's door was smashed shut. I had to climb out of the car through the back door to order! As I stood there ordering I could feel all the looks of the people around me, and these looks didn't feel so good. I wanted to stand up and announce, *"This isn't really my car! I oversee a ministry to give cars away!"* The enemy was working in that moment, but right then God showed me that I needed to deal with a heart issue I had toward money. It didn't matter what those people thought of me and my financial situation. It matters what God thinks of me.

Many of us have a heart issue that causes us to desire the approval of others and it affects how we steward different areas of our lives. For some of us, we want our possessions to make others think highly of us or fill some void. For others, maybe it's not financial at all. It's all a matter of the heart and where we find our identities.

To cultivate the heart of a good steward, we need to surrender every area of our lives to God and ask Him to show us where our hearts are out of alignment with His. Remember that everything we have belongs to God. I want my heart to belong completely to Him and I believe you want the same.

PRAYER

God, thank You so much for Your love and grace. Please reveal to me if there are any areas that I find my identity in my stuff or lack thereof. Help me to see my identity in You. I want You to have my full heart. In Jesus' name, Amen.

WHAT IS THE HOLY SPIRIT SAYING TO ME?

FOR FURTHER STUDY
Matthew 6:25–34; Hebrews 13:5–6; Colossians 3:23–24; Matthew 22:37

Day 3 | *by Jimmy Evans*

STEWARDING YOUR SPOUSE

■●▲

And the Lord said, "Who then is that faithful and wise steward, whom his master will make ruler over his household, to give them their portion of food in due season? Blessed is that servant whom his master will find so doing when he comes. Truly, I say to you that he will make him ruler over all that he has." Luke 12:42–44

As stewards, we will one day stand before God in judgment to give an account for how we have managed what is His. But did you know that also includes how we treated the *people* God has entrusted to us—our spouses and children?

One of the most basic premises of stewardship is that we are not owners—we are managers of what God owns. And we cannot own people—God owns them. Therefore, more than we steward our wealth, talents, or anything else, we are first and foremost stewards of *people* beginning with our immediate families and especially our spouses. The *things* in our lives are mere objects that exist to serve those whom God loves. The ultimate perversion of stewardship is to forsake the people in our lives—especially our spouses and children—for the sake of money, fame, or personal gain.

Instead, when we are faithful and wise stewards of God's household like Jesus talks about in Luke 12:42–44, He is pleased and promises lavish blessings in return. So how will we be judged? He will examine if our lives enhanced and bettered those around us for His sake or had a negative effect. The people around us belong to God and we are stewards responsible to treat them as He would. When we do this obediently, we are pleasing to God and will receive lavish rewards when we are called into account on the day of judgment.

The most precious gift God has given me in this life is my wife, Karen. As a young husband I dominated her, ignored her, and spoke to her harshly at times. I deeply wounded her with my careless words and uncaring behavior. At that time, I was oblivious to the stewardship I had for her as God's precious daughter. And I would have been completely unprepared to stand in account for her and how I had treated her.

But not today! One day early in our marriage, the Lord came to me and in an instant showed me how wrong I was. Now by God's grace I am His steward of Karen. And I am prepared to give an account for her and the other precious people God has entrusted to me. How about you? Are you an obedient people steward?

PRAYER

Father, I accept today that I am a steward of the people You have put into my life—especially my spouse and children. I realize they don't belong to me and I don't have the right to treat them as I wish. I surrender now as a steward of my family and the people You have put into my life. Fill me with Your grace and supernatural power to be an obedient steward. I pray that everyone around me will be bettered and blessed by the influence my life has upon theirs. In Jesus' name, Amen!

WHAT IS THE HOLY SPIRIT SAYING TO ME?

FOR FURTHER STUDY
Matthew 25:31–46; Ephesians 5:21–33; 1 John 4:7–13

4

Day 4 | *by Zach Neese*
PARENTING LIKE A STEWARD

■ ● ▲

"He will also go before Him in the spirit and power of Elijah, 'to turn the hearts of the fathers to the children,' and the disobedient to the wisdom of the just, to make ready a people prepared for the Lord." Luke 1:17

I remember that chilly winter morning almost 19 years ago—swaying in a hammock, transfixed by the perfect, sleep-pursed lips of the bundled baby who had effortlessly melted me. I held my newborn son in my hands, and I was in love. My heart felt like an overblown balloon! How could any more emotion fit inside of me? I was impossibly, inexplicably *full*!

Could this be how God feels about me? Could His heart be bursting with love for *me*? Unbelievable! And if He loves me *that* much (John 3:16), it's no wonder that He sent His Beloved Saving Son to rescue me and this little one in my arms.

Then came a sobering realization: this newborn miracle was not really mine at all. This child belonged to God! I would love and father him for a time, but the God who imagined him, created him, and purchased him with blood would Father him forever. My son was a gift that I would eventually return to the Giver. I was holding in my arms a living "talent" for which I would one day give account (Matthew 25:14–19).

We usually think of stewardship in terms of time, money, and talent, but relationships are the riches of heaven.

And if children are the treasures of the Father's house, then parenting is a powerful way God demonstrates His trust in us. He trusts us to steward our kids, and *we* have to trust *Him* to show us how.

What does it mean to parent as a steward? It means that I father "my" children as though they are not my own—to prepare them to know, love, and follow their heavenly Father forever.

Like shepherds tending our Master's flock, we teach our children to know His voice by praying and listening with them. We help them tune their ears to the truth by reading the Bible with them. We teach them the boundaries of biblical morality by leading them to submit their opinions and wills to God's opinion and will. And we protect them from the ever-present reality of wolves that want to prey upon them, use them, and consume them.

All of this requires the commitment of our greatest resource—our lives. Like Jesus, we lay down our lives, comfort, and wills over and over again to bring the children He loves to the Father. *That* is what it means to parent like a steward. It means that I invest my heart in preparing my children's hearts for God. So in days to come, when their Father calls, they will know His voice and run to Him.

PRAYER

God, thank You for the gift of my children. Help me, Father, to see them through Your eyes, to speak Your words to them, and to love them with Your heart. Please give me wisdom to steward their young lives today—to lead them in Your ways, help them hear Your voice, love Your presence, and cherish Your kingdom so they will follow You all the days of their lives. In Jesus' name, Amen.

WHAT IS THE HOLY SPIRIT SAYING TO ME?

FOR FURTHER STUDY
Deuteronomy 11:18–21; Psalms 127–128; Matthew 19:14–15; Ephesians 6:1–4; Ezekiel 16:20–22; Isaiah 45:9–12

Day 5 | *by Chelsea Seaton*
BOOM!

As iron sharpens iron, so a friend sharpens a friend.
Proverbs 27:17 (NLT)

One day I was talking with some friends when one of them said something I agreed with and instead of my response being "I agree," or simply nodding my head, I said in a firm voice, "Boom!" The look on their faces was probably the look you have right now. *Did she just say "boom"?* I had no idea where it came from. It was not a response I'd usually say in agreement, so I brushed it off and moved on. Until later that same day, I did it again! And then again, and again, until it was just something I say.

A few weeks later I was talking to a guy I regularly work with, and when I said something he agreed with, he yelled out, "Boom!" Suddenly, a lightbulb went off in my mind. *He's the reason I keep saying boom to everything.* He had rubbed off on me and I didn't even realize it!

That story is silly, but it's an example of a real biblical principle. Who you surround yourself with will influence who you are more than you can imagine. Proverbs 27:17 says, "As iron sharpens iron, so a friend sharpens a friend." Here's my question for you today. *What are you being sharpened toward?* Are you being sharpened toward the things of God, or are you being sharpened toward the world?

Have you heard the saying, "Show me your friends and I'll show you your future"? Your friends are influencing who you are today and who you will be tomorrow. You are being sharpened, and you are sharpening others. This is why it's vital that your closest friendships are with other believers. When one of us is going through a hard time, we can pray for and come alongside each other in the fight. When someone is going through a great time, we can celebrate with each other instead of being competitive or jealous like the world is.

I want to encourage you to ask the Lord, "How am I stewarding my friends, and how am I being sharpened?" If you need Christian friends, ask Him to guide you and connect you with people. Maybe He's asking you to lead and be the one who is sharpening others toward the things of God. Allow Him to speak and you will be sharpened in your faith and experience all God has for you.

Boom!

PRAYER

Father, how am I being sharpened? My desire is to know You more so please bless my friendships that we could be people who encourage one another to grow and be closer to You. Thank You for leading me and guiding me. I trust You with my friendships. In Jesus' name, Amen.

> **WHAT IS THE HOLY SPIRIT SAYING TO ME?**

FOR FURTHER STUDY
1 Corinthians 15:33; Ecclesiastes 4:9; Matthew 22:39

6

Day 6 | *by Mike Brisky*
A THOUGHTFUL MANAGER
■●▲

The Lord said, "A trustworthy and thoughtful manager who understands the ways of his master will be given a ministry of responsibility in his master's house, serving others exactly what they need at just the right time." Luke 12:42 (TPT)

Growing up, I had dreams of sinking a 10-foot putt on the last hole of a US Open golf championship to beat Jack Nicklaus, arguably the greatest golfer ever. Well, I never got a chance to play against the great Jack Nicklaus, but I did have an *opportunity* to make a 10-foot putt to win a PGA Tour Tournament.

However, I didn't make that putt, but I did take valuable lessons from my golf career into my next one. I played for seven years on the PGA Tour before the Lord opened the door for me in ministry at Gateway Church. Throughout those seven years, I went through a lot of caddies. Caddies are the people who carry a 40-pound bag for five hours or more *serving* the golfer who hired them. Unfortunately, I wasn't firing caddies because they didn't work well with me. On the contrary, it was *I* who couldn't work well with *them*. You see, I expected the caddies I hired to be knowledgeable and learn my habits and needs without me having to say a word. In other words, I wanted them to automatically be the complete package while I invested little into their lives. I didn't realize until my golf career ended and I was working at

Gateway that I had mismanaged people. I had to look at myself and say, "What am I doing?" That's when I began growing in my ability to manage and oversee people.

The gift of stewarding people is not something a person is born with; it is a talent that increases over time through your investment in your relationship with God. It should be our primary investment. Knowing that our relationship with Him is our source for being a good steward of the resources and gifts He has given us—especially people—is the key.

In Colossians 2:2, the apostle Paul explains that as we encourage people in their hearts, *they grow more* in the revelation of who God is. As we love and encourage the people with whom we work and do business, they will grow in their relationships with God. This doesn't just go for people we manage. We are called to steward our relationships with those who manage us and those we work alongside. But it can only be done through a position of humility. Just look at Joseph and his boss Potiphar in Genesis 39. While Joseph is tempted and ultimately wrongly accused by his boss, he still kept his attitude of humility even as he sat in prison. In the end, he was promoted to second in command of an entire nation.

The people we work with were put in our lives by God. To understand how to steward our relationships with them, we must first have a relationship with *Him*. Simply look at today's verse. When we understand the ways of our Master by investing in our relationship with Him, He will inspire us to be great stewards of the people He has given us in our workplace. How are you stewarding the people He has given you in your workplace?

PRAYER

Holy Spirit, help me realize more and more that the most valuable resource I have to steward in my life is people. Help me to see people the way You see them and to love them the way You love them. May my investment in my relationship with You be revealed and reflected in full measure in the relationships in my life. In Jesus' name, Amen.

WHAT IS THE HOLY SPIRIT SAYING TO ME?

FOR FURTHER STUDY
Ephesians 3:20; Colossians 2:1–3; Acts 20:28; Luke 16:1–12

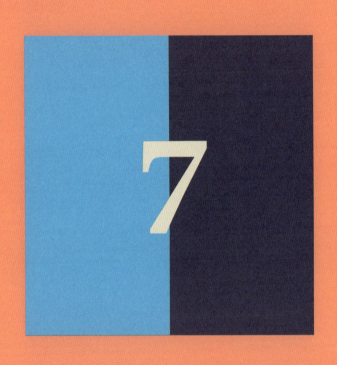

Day 7 | *by Phillip Hunter*
HONOR YOUR FAMILY

■●▲

"Honor your father and mother. Then you will live a long, full life in the land the Lord your God is giving you." Exodus 20:12 (NLT)

I am so blessed and thankful for my family, and I have the greatest parents and in-laws in the world. But no family is perfect. In the early years of our marriage, as our families were learning to relate to new in-laws, it seemed sometimes when we were together someone would say something that landed wrong. Feelings would get hurt, and intentions would be misinterpreted. We knew everyone meant well, but we all had different perspectives or ways we had done things before.

I remember a specific car ride one Sunday afternoon many years ago. My wife and I were talking about a frustration and hurt over a family situation. We realized there was going to be a day our five children would be grown and have families of their own. How would they relate to us one day? Could it be determined by the way we modeled it to our parents? We decided that day that no one would receive more grace and honor than our families, and it changed everything for us.

So what does it look like to steward your family? I believe it begins with *honor*. When you observe a family that is unified and full of love, you will notice that they honor each other. To honor means to revere, prize, and value. Honor isn't something that is merely earned but has more to do with position. I honor my family because God has entrusted them to me.

Honor begins with your parents, no matter what age you are. If you look at today's verse, you'll see it's so important to God that He lists it as the only commandment with a promise. But why honor them first? Parents are the head and focal point of a family. If the parents are honored, it will flow down to the rest of the family. And the Holy Spirit loves to move in an atmosphere of honor. Just look at Ephesians 4:29–30 (ESV):

Let no corrupting talk come out of your mouths, but only such as is good for building up, as fits the occasion, that it may give grace to those who hear. And do not grieve the Holy Spirit of God, by whom you were sealed for the day of redemption.

This passage gives instruction on how we should speak to each other to create and foster an atmosphere of honor. Next, it speaks to an emotion of the Holy Spirit. Do you realize your words make room for the Holy Spirit to move in your family? What kinds of words are you speaking and allowing to be spoken in your home?

Maybe your family is hurting today and not walking in unity. You may not even be talking. I want to encourage you to entrust them to the Lord. How do you do that? Give the Lord your attitudes, actions, and words concerning your family. If you want to steward your family well, ask the Holy Spirit to give you the ability to honor them.

PRAYER

Heavenly Father, from whom every family in heaven and on earth is named, we thank You for the family You have entrusted to us. We give You our attitudes, our actions, and our words today. Holy Spirit, help me to honor them today. In Jesus' name, Amen.

WHAT IS THE HOLY SPIRIT SAYING TO ME?

FOR FURTHER STUDY
Exodus 21:15–17; Proverbs 6:20–23

Day 8 | *by Jelani Lewis*

HEAD, SHOULDERS, KNEES, AND TOES

■●▲

Just as our bodies have many parts and each part has a special function, so it is with Christ's body. We are many parts of one body, and we all belong to each other. In his grace, God has given us different gifts for doing certain things well. Romans 12:4–6 (NLT)

Before I became a pastor, I played and coached college football. Now let me pause for a moment because when a person who is 5 feet, 6 inches, and 165 pounds at the time (married life has a way of adding pounds and muffin tops) claims to have graced the field turf as a wide receiver, the assumption is that they must have been fast. Wrong! I was able to play college ball not because I was fast, but because I was … well … scared. That's right—scared. You see, my teammates ran for the end zone. I, on the contrary, was so small that I had to run for my *life*.

One of the things you learn participating in any team sport is that each player has a specific role and for the team to be successful, everyone has to play their part. Now occasionally we find a lineman who desires to be a quarterback, the quarterback who wants to hit like a linebacker, or the linebacker who secretly fantasizes about water polo. However, at the end of the day, each team member understands that they have been uniquely wired, gifted, and built to fulfill a specific and vital function for the team.

In Romans 12:4–6, the apostle Paul writes, "Just as our bodies have many parts and each part has a special function, so it is with Christ's body. We are many parts of one body, and we all belong to each other. In His grace, God has given us different gifts for doing certain things well." In this passage, Paul is reminding us that as believers we are a part of the body of Christ. Like the hands, feet, and ears of a natural body, spiritually we each have a distinct function and unique gifts to be stewarded to serve one another.

That being said, I know what some may be tempted to think. *Sure. It's easy for Paul to encourage someone to be a good steward and use their gifts to build up the body of Christ. Paul just happened to be a writer, a speaker, a miracle worker, a tentmaker, and an intellectual. He was extremely gifted! And, that's easy for you to write, Pastor. You're ... well ... a pastor.* The great thing about this text, however, is that God is clearly not asking us to be Paul. He is not necessarily asking you to be a pastor. And he's certainly not requiring any of us to be perfect. He is simply asking us to participate, to discover and steward the abilities and passions He placed inside of us, and to use them to build up His body.

PRAYER

God thank You for the gifts, talents, and abilities that You have placed inside me. Help me to discover what they are and give me the grace to embrace and play my role within this body. In Jesus' name, Amen!

WHAT IS THE HOLY SPIRIT SAYING TO ME?

FOR FURTHER STUDY
Romans 12:1–8; 1 Corinthians 12; 1 Peter 4:10–11

Day 9 | *by Tom Lane*
YOU *ARE* A ROLE MODEL

"You are the light of the world. A city set on a hill cannot be hidden. Nor do people light a lamp and put it under a basket, but on a stand, and it gives light to all in the house. In the same way, let your light shine before others, so that they may see your good works and give glory to your Father who is in heaven." Matthew 5:14–16 (ESV)

In 1993, Nike ran a commercial that featured NBA basketball player Charles Barkley boldly declaring, "I am not a role model!" What a stark contrast Mr. Barkley's statement makes when compared to Jesus' instruction in the book of Matthew that we are to let our light shine before others, so they may see our good works and give glory to our heavenly Father.

Respect and prestige are developed from our behavior, character, commitment, and uncompromised values, and their byproduct is *influence*. If through our actions, attitudes, and communication we influence someone to exchange bad behavior for good, then our influence has been what Jesus described. It might be something little like anger turned into an act of kindness. It might be something profound like changing the way someone treats their spouse. When we believe and understand the powerful impact of influence, it causes us to carefully consider how we conduct our lives. When we learn how to steward influence properly, we find purpose for our lives with eternal benefits.

In 1969 I saw a Christian athlete stand up at a church to talk about his relationship with Jesus. He talked in personal, relational, and nonreligious terms—very different from my religious perspective of God. When he finished, he made a simple offer, "If you would like to know more about a relationship with God, meet me down here in front of the auditorium." I was impacted by what I saw and heard, and I stepped out to meet him down front as he suggested. Not only did I meet him, but I prayed to receive Jesus Christ as my Lord and Savior. I met God and my whole life changed.

Only heaven will reveal the full impact of this athlete's influence. He introduced me to a personal relationship with God rather than religious knowledge of Him—with impact on my purpose, character, morals, career, marriage, children and grandchildren, and friendships. The light of his influence glorified God and drew me to the light of His love and purpose.

Have you considered the influence of your life? Are you hiding the light of your influence for God? Let your light shine! Be an influence for others to see, and their lives will be impacted.

PRAYER

Lord, thank You for Your love and abiding presence in my life. Help me to live and act in such a way that others are influenced to seek You! In Jesus' name, Amen.

WHAT IS THE HOLY SPIRIT SAYING TO ME?

FOR FURTHER STUDY

John 13:34–35; 1 Corinthians 15:33; Proverbs 14:7

10

Day 10 | *by Tim Ross*
JESUS' FARMING ADVICE
■ ● ▲

"Behold, a sower went out to sow. And as he sowed, some seed fell by the wayside; and the birds came and devoured them. Some fell on stony places, where they did not have much earth; and they immediately sprang up because they had no depth of earth. But when the sun was up they were scorched, and because they had no root they withered away. And some fell among thorns, and the thorns sprang up and choked them. But others fell on good ground and yielded a crop: some a hundredfold, some sixty, some thirty." Matthew 13:3–8

Have you ever heard the term low-hanging fruit? It refers to fruit that's easy to harvest. You can walk right up to it and it's ready and easy to pick. Looking back, that's how I could describe myself at age 20. See, I grew up in one of the most warm and loving homes you can imagine. I hit the lottery when it came to parents. They had structured our home to be a safe environment where you could be honest and transparent, but I couldn't operate in that world, and I'll tell you why.

At age eight, I was sexually abused by a neighbor across the street, and I decided to keep it a secret from my parents. This secret destroyed me from the inside out, causing me to struggle with addiction and insecurity. One day when I was 19, my mother discovered and confronted my addiction, and that's when I finally told her my secret. I found out that she and my father had both suffered the same abuse as children. In that moment of truth, the Holy Spirit began to work in my life, and six months later I stood up from my seat in the back of my parents' church, and I said, "I give up. I need to give my life to God right now."

See what I mean by low-hanging fruit? No one even had to *invite* me to get saved. My parents had sowed a seed in me decades before, and I was ready for the harvest.

There's a mistake we tend to make when we think about evangelism. We only think about the harvest—that salvation moment—when there's an entire agricultural process that's involved in evangelism. We forget about sowing (sharing the gospel) and watering (treating someone with kindness and love and praying for them) because they don't seem as exciting as harvesting. However, God has given all of us the gifts of sowing and watering as well as harvesting, even though you may be most comfortable in one or another.

In fact, take a look at the parable of the sower in today's verse. Jesus uses it to instruct us to sow the seed of the gospel everywhere we go. If we take His parable literally, it's *really terrible* farming advice, because the sower doesn't care whether the ground is thorny or stony—he just throws it out everywhere!

So many of us are worried about making the seed stick or explaining our faith in a way that people can *get* it. The truth is, those are the jobs of the Holy Spirit. Our job is simply to sow our seed. Just like the sower in the parable, take a handful and *chuck* it! And ask the Holy Spirit, "What is my assignment today? Am I sowing, watering, or harvesting?" Chances are, as you steward your role in the agricultural process of evangelism, you might do a little of each. It's all a matter of listening to His voice and following where He leads as you sow, water, and harvest.

PRAYER

Lord, thank You for giving me a role in bringing people to You. Give me a heart for the lost around me and give me boldness and love as I share the gospel with them. In Jesus' name, Amen.

> **WHAT IS THE HOLY SPIRIT SAYING TO ME?**

FOR FURTHER STUDY
John 6:44; Luke 14:23; Mark 16:15

Day 11 | *by Jimmy Evans*

THE STEWARDSHIP OF SUBMISSION

■ ● ▲

Obey those who rule over you, and be submissive, for they watch out for your souls, as those who must give account. Let them do so with joy and not with grief, for that would be unprofitable for you. Hebrews 13:17

When I pastored at Trinity Fellowship Church in Amarillo, there was a couple in our church who brought me a great deal of grief. They were both in leadership when I became the senior pastor, and the wife was on our staff. I can't remember one instance when they followed a directive given to them without resistance, attitude, arrogance, and spreading their disagreement to those around them and causing division.

Finally after several years of trying to patiently and lovingly lead them, I had enough and let them know if they couldn't submit, they couldn't be in leadership or on staff. Their response was predictable. They left the church and started one of their own. They called many leaders and members of Trinity and told them blatant lies about me and what I had said and done and invited them to join their new group.

Their church ultimately grew to around 200 people. It wasn't a large percentage of our congregation—but the suffering they caused was disproportionately great. I cannot tell you the pain they caused me, my family, our church, and our community. And within a year or so, their church was no more.

Being in authority is serious business with God, and it is a matter of stewardship. People don't belong to us—they belong to God. And anyone we oversee is God's child, and we will give an account to Him for our authority in his or her life.

But submission is also a form of stewardship. Notice in today's Scripture that it directs those under authority to make their overseer's job a "joy" and not a "grief." The writer of Hebrews then tells us if we make their job difficult it will be "unprofitable" for us. The word unprofitable in the Greek language means "no reward" but by implication can also mean "exceedingly harmful."

I will stand one day before God and give an account for the difficult couple I told you about. I love them and forgive them, but I will tell Jesus the truth. They were a grief to me and made my job much harder. But I will also give account for the many thousands of dear saints who have lifted my hands and heart and served Jesus alongside me. The grief I've experienced pales in comparison to the joy that has been given to me by the sweetest people on earth at Trinity Fellowship Church and at Gateway Church.

Whether you're in a position of authority or you're under authority (and we all are!), let's commit ourselves to being better stewards for God so we can give Him a joyful account on the day of judgment.

PRAYER

Father, I submit my heart to You and all of the authority figures in my life. I repent of pride, independence, and rebellion. I realize You have placed authority in my life to protect and direct me. I commit to submitting to anyone with authority over me and making their role in my life a joy. Also, for all of those under my authority, I am reminded that I will give an account to You one day for how I used my role in their lives. Most of all, I submit to You as my Lord and Master and commit my life to being a wise and faithful steward for Your kingdom. In Jesus' name, Amen.

WHAT IS THE HOLY SPIRIT SAYING TO ME?

FOR FURTHER STUDY
Romans 13:1–7; Luke 19:11–27; Ephesians 6:1–9

12

Day 12 | *by Preston Morrison*
WHO'S THE BOSS?

■●▲

"Whatever you do, work at it with all your heart, as working for the Lord, not for human masters." Colossians 3:23 (NIV)

When I first joined the staff at Gateway Church almost 20 years ago, I was answering directly to Pastor Robert. I was 22 years old and had much to learn. I remember the day he said, "Preston, you're not always going to answer to me. You will go on to have other bosses who oversee you here. They're not going to see everything you do for this church, and I won't see everything you do for this church either. But don't let that be your motivation. Remember that even though I don't see everything, God does, and you work for Him, not me."

Have you ever noticed we tend to step up our game when we feel someone important is watching? I catch my boys doing this all the time. I'll tell them to brush their teeth before bed, and when they don't think I'm watching, it's like the toothbrush barely touches their teeth and they're finished. A funny thing happens, though, when they realize I'm watching them. They practically become gold-medalist teeth brushers.

What would you change about the way you work if you realized you don't work for yourself, or for your boss, but for the Lord? And what would you do differently if you realized He was always watching? Would you work harder? Would you show up earlier? Would you spend company money differently? You probably would and that's great. But rather than changing these behaviors directly, consider the following suggestions as supplements to your changes: be more grateful each day God gives you at your job no matter how hard or bad it gets, and make the place where God put you a better place for all to be.

God is a really great "boss." The question is would God say you make a really great employee?

PRAYER

Lord, thank You for the opportunity to work where you have placed me. Give me a heart for those around me, gratitude for my job even on difficult days, and a mindset that You're my boss. In Jesus' name, Amen.

> **WHAT IS THE HOLY SPIRIT SAYING TO ME?**

FOR FURTHER STUDY
1 Corinthians 10:31; Ephesians 6:7; Colossians 3:17

Day 13 | *by S. George Thomas*
A PLATFORM OF INFLUENCE

■●▲

So we are Christ's ambassadors .... 2 Corinthians 5:20 (NLT)

Once upon a time, there was a good king who ruled over a kingdom of light, love, and peace. One day, the king commissioned an ambassador to represent him in a foreign land ruled by a cruel dictator—a kingdom of darkness, torn apart by strife. The good king wanted the people of the other country to know he welcomed them to enjoy the safety of his land. As the ambassador prepared to depart, the king reminded her they could *always* call on him whenever they needed help.

Do you know who that ambassador is? It's you! The day you asked Jesus to be your Savior and Lord, you became a citizen of another kingdom. But beyond that, you became an ambassador of that kingdom and its King, with the privilege and responsibility of representing Him in this world (2 Corinthians 5:17–20).

The Greek word for "ambassador" in the New Testament is *presbeuo*, which shares the same root as "presbyter"—a word used to describe church leaders. So while you may not be a pastor, you *are* an ambassador. And just as our pastors are accountable before God for how they steward the words they speak from their platforms, each of us is accountable to God for how we steward *our* circles of influence—including what we share on various social media platforms. Because for better or for worse, social media is a significant platform of influence.

Think about this. The average American spends 135 minutes a day on social media. This means over a lifetime, we'll spend five years and four months on social media compared to only a year and three months socializing with friends and family in real life! But as ambassadors of Jesus, our social media platforms are not *ours*. They are a part of the sphere of influence God has entrusted to us. And you and I are each called to steward that sphere of influence wisely—to be salt and light (Matthew 5:13–16).

Now hear me out ... I'm *not* suggesting the only things you should post on social media are Scriptures, sermon quotes, or what God's spoken to you that day. A lot of what we see and post on social media is just sheer fun—and fun is great! It's great to post pics from an awesome meal you had on a night out with your spouse. And wanting to stay in touch with the ongoing daily lives of your family and friends is wonderful as well.

What I *am* suggesting is this—what if you pause for a moment before you post or share anything and ask yourself these questions: *Is this post life-giving?*

Does it create peace? Am I posting this comment out of kindness and love? Does it spark joy, laughter, or even just a smile? Am I bringing encouragement and hope?

If you can confidently answer "yes" to any of these questions, then rest assured you are representing your King well.

PRAYER

Father, thank You for giving me the privilege to represent You in every area of life. I want the things I post to bring encouragement and life to my sphere of influence on social media. So I'm asking You: Will You give me wisdom and help me be sensitive to what You want me to post today? In all that I do, I want You to be glorified. In Jesus' name, Amen.

WHAT IS THE HOLY SPIRIT SAYING TO ME?

FOR FURTHER STUDY
2 Corinthians 5:17–20 (NLT); Matthew 5:13–16 (NIV); Jeremiah 15:19 (NLT); 2 Corinthians 10:13 (ESV)

Day 14 | *by Thomas Miller*
THE CREATIVE INVITE

"For since the creation of the world His invisible attributes are clearly seen, being understood by the things that are made." Romans 1:20

In the beginning there was nothing. Absolutely nothing. Other than the divine God himself, there was nothing. Not even time.

And then He spoke. From the heights of His power and glory and from the depths of His multifaceted, multidimensional imagination and ingenuity, He created. "Let there be … ." And there was. And it was good.

From the majestic wonder and beauty of the vast expanse of the universe to the refraction of light displaying the colors of the spectrum on the surface of the oceans. From the living creatures freely roaming the earth to the tiniest of molecules giving microscopic order and dimension to all matter, and from all that is seen to all that is unseen—He created. And it was good.

Beautiful. Breathtaking. Awe-inspiring. The creation reflected its Creator in all of His splendor. But then, as if to show that He actually was saving His deepest, most profound creativity for last, He designed something that actually looked, felt, thought, and talked like Him. Something in His very image. Something that would have authority and creativity.

He spoke. He created. Man became.

One of the aspects of the creation story that I find so fascinating is that in the midst of all the creativity God displayed, He actually chose to not fully finish the job. In fact, He let man in on the creative process.

"Out of the ground the Lord God formed every beast of the field and every bird of the air, and brought them to Adam to see what he would call them. And whatever Adam called each living creature, that was its name." Genesis 2:19

God himself could have named each animal and told Adam what each one was to be named. But He stewarded that creative process to Adam. In fact, I love how this verse shows that God validated Adam's creativity by saying "whatever Adam called each living creature, that was its name." God didn't say to Adam, "Nice try, but those names just aren't good enough. You really need to step it up. You're just not as creative as I am." No, God clearly invited Adam into the creative process and then validated him in his efforts. I believe God is still inviting us into His creative process today.

As ones who have been formed in the image of God—the ultimate creative genius, we have the ability to be creative and exercise ingenuity in every aspect of our lives, whether at home, in business, or at play. And when our creativity is coupled with God's presence, the results can truly be astounding. What we make can bring glory to God.

Let's steward the creativity God has given us so we can more clearly see His glory on display in our lives.

PRAYER

Father, I ask that You help me see that You've invited me into Your creative process. Help me to see ways that I could be creative and show Your glory on display in my life. In Jesus' name, Amen.

WHAT IS THE HOLY SPIRIT SAYING TO ME?

FOR FURTHER STUDY
Genesis 1:27; Psalm 104:24; Ephesians 2:10

15

Day 15 | *by Allan Kelsey*
GOD-SIZED INVITATIONS

Then Jacob was left alone; and a Man wrestled with him until the breaking of day. Now when He saw that He did not prevail against him, He touched the socket of his hip; and the socket of Jacob's hip was out of joint as He wrestled with him. And He said, "Let Me go, for the day breaks." But he said, "I will not let You go unless You bless me!"
Genesis 32:24–26

When I was growing up, I wanted a motorcycle in the worst possible way. I dreamt about it, I had posters on my wall, and I bought motorcycle magazines. I bargained with God to get one, I reasoned and pleaded with my parents, but in the end, no motorcycle for me.

At the same time in my life, I was starting to compete more seriously in swimming meets and work harder in my daily training. My race times got faster and soon I began to realize this talent might lead to bigger opportunities.

Even at 12 years old, I recognized that I was leveraging a God-given ability and felt somehow invited to steward the talent and follow the invitations God provided through it. At the conclusion of my South African high school career, I received a scholarship to the United States to fully explore the extent of the talent I had been given.

It was about this time that I began to more deeply understand the power and difference of a *me*-sized dream and a *God*-sized invitation. My motorcycle dream was object-focused and self-serving, but God's invitation was to be the strongest version of myself, for His sake and His destiny over me. What I learned is that chasing a self-serving dream is not necessarily wrong, but it is limited in its scope. However, when God invites you to collaborate with Him in the strongest contribution your life could make on earth, then you are being invited to destiny! *Your* destiny.

In this pursuit, lessons of perseverance, focus, stamina, and determination will surface. They will test you beyond what you think you can endure, so you can learn that there truly is *more* in you than you thought. These proofs are not for God to know if you've got it, they are for you to see that you've got it.

This is why God's invitations (the aspirations He places on our lives) are worthy of our highest efforts, rather than the self-centered dreams about motorcycles. Because in these efforts, you will make your highest contribution to the world and along the way discover the strongest version of yourself.

In today's Scripture, God picks a fight with Jacob and wrestles with him. When Jacob realizes he is wrestling with his destiny, he presses in to get a *me*-sized dream—a blessing from the Man of God. God tests him further by touching Jacob's hip and still Jacob would not let Him go. As you continue reading, Jacob pleads and bargains with God to give him the thing he dreams of—a blessing, a sort of self-serving thing. In reply, God invites Jacob to a new destiny and confirms it by changing his identity. God did not need to wrestle with Jacob to learn something about him. Instead, God needed to wrestle with Jacob because Jacob needed to learn something about how to pursue God-sized invitations!

As you look at your life, are you pursuing me-sized dreams or God-sized invitations? I want to encourage you to respond to God's invitations in your life. He's given each of us a destiny and purpose, and it's up to us to use the tools, talents, and gifts He's given us to achieve them for His glory and kingdom.

PRAYER

God, thank You for the purpose and destiny that You have given me. Show me the invitations You've given me and help me to steward my time and efforts to respond to Your purpose for my life. I don't want to waste my time on my own dreams, but I want to pursue the dreams You have for me. In Jesus' name, Amen.

WHAT IS THE HOLY SPIRIT SAYING TO ME?

FOR FURTHER STUDY
Genesis 32:22–29; Ephesians 2:10; 1 Peter 4:10

16

Day 16 | *by Robert Morris*
TWO LEGS REQUIRED

■●▲

Wealth is a crown for the wise; the effort of fools yields only foolishness.
Proverbs 14:24 (NLT)

Several years ago, I preached a series at Gateway on *The Blessed Life*, which is all about living a life of generosity. After the series was finished, I noticed a couple in our church who became extremely generous with their finances. I could tell the message of *The Blessed Life* had really impacted their lives, as it had many others before, including my own. Their generosity was a blessing to many people around them, but then one day it just stopped. Later they came to me and said that while they loved being generous with their finances, they weren't managing them in a way that allowed them to continue a lifestyle of generosity. Let me say this a different way. They weren't *stewarding* their finances well. They were buried in credit card debt and were living well beyond their means. As they described their situation, I thought, *How can you give what you don't have?*

This came as a surprise to me because when I wrote *The Blessed Life*, I assumed everyone would know they had to first manage their finances in a way that would allow them to be lavishly generous. However, as I began to see more and more people faced with the same situation, I realized *The Blessed Life* was actually part two of a message about generosity. Part one, covered in my book *Beyond Blessed*, sets the foundation of stewardship.

You see, a life of blessing walks on two legs—one is generosity and the other is financial stewardship. If you try to walk on the generosity leg without using the stewardship leg, you'll be walking in circles. The Bible clearly charges us to be stewards of all God has given us. In Genesis 2:15, God put Adam in the Garden of Eden to "tend and keep it," even going as far to tell Adam and Eve to "be fruitful and multiply; fill the earth and subdue it," in Genesis 1:28. And the truth is, the stewardship leg is the vital *first* leg you need to have in place, so you have the ability to live a life of generosity.

Here's wonderful news: the ability to wisely manage wealth and material possessions is not a talent with which you're gifted at birth. It's a skill. This means it can be taught and learned. It is a form of wisdom, and the book of Proverbs wouldn't encourage us to "get wisdom" (Proverbs 4:7) if it weren't available to everyone with enough humility to receive it.

This may mean you need to look at your finances and find ways you can cut back, so you can have more discretionary funds with which to be generous. Or maybe it means working as hard as you can to eliminate consumer debt or other bad debt from your life, so you can live a lifestyle of blessing others.

When you look at your life, do you see the leg of generosity stronger than the leg of stewardship? Do you find yourself walking in circles? If so, ask the Holy Spirit to show you how you can become a better steward of your finances and then obey what He says. It's then you can truly live beyond blessed.

PRAYER

Lord, thank You for Your generosity toward me and for the opportunity to be generous to others. Please show me how to become a better steward of my finances, so I can give more generously wherever You lead me. In Jesus' name, Amen.

WHAT IS THE HOLY SPIRIT SAYING TO ME?

FOR FURTHER STUDY
Genesis 2:15; Romans 13:8

17

Day 17 | *by Stacy Burnett*
LETTING GO

"Look at the birds of the air, for they neither sow nor reap nor gather into barns; yet your heavenly Father feeds them. Are you not of more value than they?" Matthew 6:26

Several years ago, my husband and I had a series of unexpected expenses pile up. Before we knew it, we'd racked up some debt. As we talked about ways to make extra money and pay it off, I suggested we sell some of our belongings. We'd be simplifying while also making money on the side; it seemed like a win-win. But as we prayed about it, we sensed the Lord leading us to *give* our things away and trust *Him* to provide for us.

At first, this was a hard concept for me to grasp. I knew all our possessions belonged to the Lord, and we're called to be wise stewards with both our belongings and money, so why would we *give* things away without asking anything in return?

What I came to realize is I had a fear of letting go—even of the smallest things—because I was unsure I'd be able to get them if I needed them again. I also realized I had adopted a mindset of "get as much as I can now, because I may not be able to get it later!" So, I bought and kept things I didn't need—just in case. Over time, our closets started to look more like storage units than places to hang our clothes.

When we're reluctant to part with our possessions because of what *might* happen in the future, what we often believe deep down is: *"God, I can't trust You enough to take care of me."* That's actually a spirit of poverty. We allow ourselves to be bound by fear, when God wants us to walk and live in freedom and peace.

I recently saw a picture that beautifully illustrates this point. In it, a little girl is standing in front of Jesus clutching a little stuffed teddy bear in her arms. With tears in her eyes, she says, "But I love it!" All the while Jesus is gently telling her, "Just trust Me." What the little girl can't see is Jesus holding a *huge* stuffed teddy bear behind His back. He's just waiting for her to trust Him, so He can give her more than she could ever imagine!

I now know God wanted us to give our things away rather than sell them, because He wanted us to depend on *Him* and put our trust in *His* goodness and faithfulness to provide for us. After we obeyed the Lord and let things go, He provided opportunities for us to make extra money, and we were able to pay off all our debt. Let me tell you, there's so much freedom and hope in obeying the Lord—even when it doesn't make sense—rather than letting fear drive you into doing it your way.

What are you holding onto that you need to let go? God loves you and wants to provide the very best for you. Just as He provided (and still provides) for us more than we could have ever imagined, He can do the same for you. You simply need to trust and obey Him, and then get ready to experience the abundance of His love and provision.

PRAYER

Lord, help me to remember that everything I have belongs to You. Give me the wisdom I need to be a good and faithful steward of all You've given me. I choose to put my full trust in You and believe You will provide for my every need. Thank You for loving me and taking care of me and my family, today and always. In Jesus' name, Amen.

> **WHAT IS THE HOLY SPIRIT SAYING TO ME?**

FOR FURTHER STUDY

Psalm 46:1; 1 John 4:18; 1 Timothy 6:17; Ephesians 3:20

18

Day 18 | *by James Morris*
HAVE YOU BEEN FAITHFUL?

■●▲

"And if you have not been faithful in what is another man's, who will give you what is your own?" Luke 16:12

Have you ever heard the saying, "The rich get richer and the poor get poorer"? Well, that principle is actually biblical. People increase where they are good stewards and decrease where they are poor stewards. Often money flows out of the hands of those who don't steward it well and into the hands of those who do. The parable of the talents in Matthew 25:14–30 is a great example of this.

If you want more of something, whether it's influence, money, work position, or better health, you must look at how you're stewarding what you already have. Another word for stewarding is managing. If you hired someone to manage your stuff and they handled it all the exact same way you have, would you be pleased with their work? Would you want to promote them?

I was once helping mediate between two couples who had a conflict. One family was renting a house from the other family. However, the renter was not taking care of the house, nor were they paying on time. This was a heart issue. I talked through many biblical principles as we worked toward a resolution. I remember asking the renter, "Would you like to have your own house one day?" They said, "Oh yes, absolutely!" I told them they hadn't set themselves up to do this. "What?" they said surprised.

I went on to read Luke 16:12, "And if you have not been faithful in what is another man's, who will give you what is your own?" I pointed out that they weren't taking very good care of the other family's house and that if they wanted to one day have a house of their own, taking care of the house they already lived in would be a good place to start.

We can take this principle a step further. Remember God owns everything, and if you'd like to see an increase in a certain area of your life, simply look at the way you're managing what He's already given you. Are you the kind of steward He's looking for?

PRAYER

Father in heaven, thank You for loving me, choosing me, and calling me Your child. Please help me to take care of the things You've entrusted to me. Help me become a better manager who honors You. In Jesus' name, Amen.

WHAT IS THE HOLY SPIRIT SAYING TO ME?

FOR FURTHER STUDY
Matthew 25:14-30; 1 Corinthians 4:2; Luke 12:42–46; Proverbs 3:27

Day 19 | *by David Thompson*
TALENTS AND SPIRITUAL GIFTS

As each one has received a gift, minister it to one another, as good stewards of the manifold grace of God. If anyone speaks, let him speak as the oracles of God. If anyone ministers, let him do it as with the ability which God supplies, that in all things God may be glorified through Jesus Christ, to whom belong the glory and the dominion forever and ever. Amen. 1 Peter 4:10–11

During the weekend services at Gateway Church, I like to walk up and down the two main aisles at the Southlake Campus. I'll arrive 30 minutes early to catch up with the people I've met on previous weekends and meet first-time guests. Growing up, I didn't understand why I enjoy this so much, but as I've gotten older, I've realized God has actually given me a special talent to easily connect and engage with people. I'm always looking to make eye contact with someone and hoping to spark a conversation.

One of the beautiful things about being a part of a healthy church family is seeing the different natural talents and supernatural spiritual gifts on display. I use my gift to engage someone new, but that's just one piece of the puzzle. My friend Susie, who volunteers as an usher, uses her gift of connecting people to make sure they find a friendly person to sit with. There are others who use their gifts to usher in the presence of God in worship or pray with people at the altar. All of these natural talents and spiritual gifts come from the Lord, and they all bring glory to God through Jesus Christ.

When I step back and look at the hundreds of volunteers serving each weekend at Gateway, greeting at the door, serving coffee, answering questions, interpreting foreign languages, running the cameras, ministering to children, worshipping from the platform, and pastoring people, I'm overwhelmed by how wonderfully unique each person is and how masterfully God has brought us together for His glory. Every person has been given gifts, and the whole body of Christ is impacted when you discover them and use them to serve others.

The Bible tells us that God gives us our abilities, has good works set up in advance for us to do, and rewards us both here on earth and in heaven for being faithful with these talents and spiritual gifts. If you truly recognize God as the owner of all things, then it will be easy to ask the Holy Spirit what He wants you to do with the unique gifts He's entrusted to you.

As you go to Him daily for insight on how and when to use these gifts, you'll develop a deeper and more intimate relationship with God. The heart of a steward is to grow closer to the Master, using every resource to honor His desires and have the maximum impact for His kingdom. Will you commit to listening for the voice of the Holy Spirit today?

PRAYER

Father, thank You for depositing natural talents and spiritual gifts inside of me. Thank You for empowering me with Your Holy Spirit to use these gifts to impact the lives of others. Allow me to hear You more clearly so I can steward every gift according to Your Word. In Jesus' name, Amen.

WHAT IS THE HOLY SPIRIT SAYING TO ME?

FOR FURTHER STUDY
Ephesians 2:10; Proverbs 22:29; Matthew 5:14–16; 1 Corinthians 12:1–11

20

Day 20 | *by Mallory Bassham*
THE MOST IMPORTANT THING
■●▲

"Seek the Kingdom of God above all else, and live righteously, and he will give you everything you need." Matthew 6:33 (NLT)

On a recent vacation I made a very difficult decision. I decided to delete Facebook and Instagram from my phone, and I turned off my email. I know what you're thinking—how courageous! But seriously, the decision to avoid distraction and be present turned out to be a good one. It resulted in richer conversations and deeper awareness and understanding of the beauty that surrounded me on my trip. I can't imagine what I'd have missed had I stayed "plugged in."

I had to make staying present a priority because I know that if I'm not intentional with my time—even my time *off*—it will simply disappear right before my eyes. And I've learned that one of the secrets of successful people is prioritizing time—something that is more and more difficult to do in today's culture. Whether at work or home, there is always something to do. And to make matters worse, we have an increasing dependence on technology, which allows every fact, direction, and picture to be at our fingertips. There are so many priorities competing for our time, and it's up to us to decide where we give our attention.

When I read the parable of the talents in Matthew 25:14–30, there is a clear picture of this principle. Focused attention to what you have in your hand will give you forward momentum. In the story, a man gave three of his servants talents or goods. Two of the servants wisely increased their talents, while the other one simply ignored his by burying it. I don't know about you, but I don't want to ignore what God has put in my hands. I want to decide what is important and work hard to develop it, whether it be my relationship with God, my family, or my career. If we are faithful to develop what He's given us, He'll respond by giving us more. So we can rest assured that we can prepare for more if we are attentive to prioritize and steward what we have.

Maybe there are too many things fighting to take priority in your life. Perhaps there are some things that are taking your attention from what's truly important. Right where you are, ask God to show you your priorities. If you'll submit your goals and plans to the Lord and prioritize your life around His plan for you, you will see incredible growth and experience rich moments along the way.

PRAYER

Lord, thank You for putting good things in my life. Show me what's important and correct me where I've gotten my priorities out of order. I put my trust in You for the goals and dreams I have. Help me to stay focused on what is important to You, because that's what's important to me too. In Jesus' name, Amen.

> **WHAT IS THE HOLY SPIRIT SAYING TO ME?**

FOR FURTHER STUDY
Micah 6:8; Psalm 37:23; Proverbs 3:5–6

21

Day 21 | *by Mary Jo Pierce*
REFRAME YOUR DAY
■●▲

In the early morning, while it was still dark, Jesus got up, left the house, and went away to a secluded place, and was praying there.
Mark 1:35 (NASB)

There's a familiar adage you might have heard, "Early to bed, early to rise, makes a man healthy, wealthy, and wise." This saying has never applied to me in the natural. I was born minutes after midnight and from that day until now, I've been a night owl. That was all fine until I started kindergarten. I was *not* one of those people who could wake up, say a cheery good morning, and go. Then when I began my career as a stewardess in the '60s and '70s, I had a 4 am wake-up call for an airplane that waits for no one. But then, my spirit was awakened to the love of Jesus in 1976, and He issued a morning invitation to meet with Him.

Today's verse is special to me because when I first read it, it was like an invitation to follow His example and begin meeting with God first thing in the morning. Despite my love for staying up late, I accepted His invitation and began looking at the changes I'd need to make and the prices I'd need to pay to allow God to reframe my 24 hours. I fasted staying up later than 10 pm and I started getting up before the sun. I created a meeting place—my prayer chair with my Bible, journal, and pen.

I learned through trial and error what works for me: it begins with praise, continues with the Word, and ends with prayer. I have determined that it's not a time for studying, memorizing Scripture, or prayer for all that concerns me. Instead, it's just a time for God and me. It's a time to orient my heart for the day, to set my compass on His north, to set my affections on Him, and to be fed today's manna through Scripture and listen to His voice. Then I pray, talk about what's on my heart, and commune with Him.

We were all created to do this very thing—commune with God. And when we set aside time first thing in the morning to meet with Him, we are reorienting our days to be centered around Him. There's no better way to begin our day than to sense Him say, "Well done, have a good day," when we leave our meeting place with Him.

PRAYER

Father, Jesus, Holy Spirit, good morning. I'm grateful it's important to You that I spend the first part of my day with You, so I will steward my time to meet You then. Please strengthen me, give me strategy, and grace my calendar to truly put first things first—You. In Jesus' name, Amen.

> **WHAT IS THE HOLY SPIRIT SAYING TO ME?**

FOR FURTHER STUDY
Matthew 6:6; Psalms 143:8, 119:147; Exodus 33:7–11

22

Day 22 | *by Mike Foltynski*
I GIVE UP

■●▲

Commit everything you do to the Lord. Trust him, and he will help you.
Psalm 37:5 (NLT)

I didn't have much growing up. My family situation was dysfunctional, and my high school career was even worse. But when I fell into a basketball scholarship at a junior college and then a university, something clicked in my brain. I became extremely driven. After college, I felt the need to prove to myself and to others that I could be successful. I took it upon myself to determine what success looked like, and in my mind, it was career driven. I started working with a management firm with good growth opportunities, and I always stayed focused on that next achievement or promotion, but I realized I was never satisfied. In fact, I became physically ill.

One Sunday when we started attending Gateway 12 years ago, my wife and I were leaving church and I ended up in the emergency room. It was a panic attack induced by stress. I was burning the candle at both ends and my body couldn't keep up with my desire to be "successful." The doctor told me I needed to figure out how to lower my stress, but I couldn't figure out how to do it. One night in my home I said, "God I don't know how to solve this problem, and I give up." From that point forward, my life began to change, and it all came from giving God control of my time each day.

As I look around, I see so many others with the same problem I had. We tend to burn the candle at both ends and even brag about how much we work. Why do so many of us live unbalanced and unhealthy lives? Maybe you are reading this, and you're exhausted like I was. In the way I cried out to God, I encourage you to do the same. Relinquish the control of your days to the One who truly has control. Declare that you want Him to lead your life. Declare that you need His help. Start committing everything you do to Him. Start trusting His promises over your life.

I believe that when you start following His instructions, amazing things will start to happen. You will care less how you are perceived by those around you. You will start saying no to requests for your time. You will start eliminating things in your life that do not produce fruit. And you will stop worrying about the things you can't control and start focusing on the One that counts. I encourage you to become a steward of the hours that God has given you. Trust Him, and He will help you.

PRAYER

Lord, I pray that You would help me stop living my life and start living Your life. I ask You to forgive me for not trusting You with the hours You have given me. Show me how to steward the hours I have and live a full, rich life filled with Your presence. In Jesus' name, Amen.

WHAT IS THE HOLY SPIRIT SAYING TO ME?

FOR FURTHER STUDY
Ephesians 5:15–17; Joshua 1:8; John 15:5; Matthew 6:34

23

Day 23 | *by Josh Morris*
REDEEM THE EARTH

■ ● ▲

Once, on being asked by the Pharisees when the kingdom of God would come, Jesus replied, "The coming of the kingdom of God is not something that can be observed, nor will people say, 'Here it is,' or 'There it is,' because the kingdom of God is in your midst."
Luke 17:20–21 (NIV)

"Don't worry, it's just a rental," I yelled as we descended down a rocky path in a small SUV that was beginning to make new and interesting sounds. We came up on an old mining town in Colorado with limited roads as we made our way to our next adventure. It was a small town, the kind where the locals can tell you're a stranger right away, and the feeling of being an outsider was clear to us and them. This feeling is familiar to everyone who has ever traveled—the excitement of discovering new lands but the unmistakable, nagging feeling of being slightly out of place.

Many times these themes are used to describe us as Christians. We are here in this temporary, fallen world, and our real home is somewhere off in the floating clouds with streets of gold and mansions for everyone, and if we can just hold off a little longer, then we can get there one day. The truth is, this view of heaven is damaging and not what the Bible teaches. We aren't just here on earth to wait for heaven. We can't simply leave this place trashed and depleted as we wait for our *real* home. God created the earth and placed us, whom He created in His image, here for a purpose. And just like He wants to redeem us, He wants to redeem the earth—and He wants to do so through you and me. With that in mind, does your stewardship of the earth redeem it or damage it?

Let's take a moment to reverse the common, flawed thinking I mentioned above. Instead of believing that we are guests in this flawed place, let's remember that God placed us here to be the image bearers of His goodness and grace. Do our actions and how we treat the earth reflect this truth, or do we treat it like "just a rental"? It is owned by God and given to us as caretakers so let's treat it as such. We are co-laborers in this land, not visitors, sent here by God Himself to bring the kingdom of heaven to earth.

PRAYER

Lord, thank You that Your kingdom is here now and not some other distant place. Make me an image bearer of Your goodness and grace in the way that I steward the earth. Help me to take better care of it as I follow You. In Jesus' name, Amen.

WHAT IS THE HOLY SPIRIT SAYING TO ME?

FOR FURTHER STUDY
Psalm 95:4–5; John 1:3

24

Day 24 | *by Robert Morris*
TAKE CARE OF YOUR TEMPLE

■ ● ▲

"Do you not know that your body is the temple of the Holy Spirit who is in you, whom you have from God, and you are not your own? For you were bought at a price; therefore glorify God in your body and in your spirit, which are God's." 1 Corinthians 6:19–20

Are there things you don't like about your body? I think almost every person has something they'd like to change. Growing up, I was ashamed of my body because I was very skinny. It's why I hated physical education. My legs were skinny, and the gym shorts we wore only brought more attention to them. The label inside read, "One size fits all," but it was a lie.

Even after I became a believer (and wasn't quite so skinny anymore), I still didn't appreciate my body and there were things I wanted to change. I knew it was "the temple of the Holy Spirit," but it took a near-death experience for me to realize that my negative thoughts about my body had opened a door for the enemy to attack me.

On a trip to Australia in 2013, I spoke 10 times in 72 hours and ended up in the hospital after having a bad reaction to a migraine pill and losing a lot of blood. My routine at the time was taking medicine for whatever caused me pain and pushing through rather than slowing down, listening to my body, and resting. So when I did this in Australia, my body shut down. The Lord used this ordeal to show me all the ways I had mistreated—and even *hated*—my own body. When we don't treat our bodies as the temple of the Holy Spirit, it can open doors in our lives for the enemy to destroy us.

Are you being a good steward of your health? Are you taking care of your body? The Bible says in Ephesians 5:29, "For no one ever hated his own flesh, but nourishes and cherishes it, just as the Lord does the church." If you aren't taking care of yourself, the Holy Spirit's expression through you will be limited, and you won't be able to accomplish all God wants you to accomplish. There were several times in my life when I could have died because I wasn't taking care of my body. I don't want to leave this earth prematurely and miss fulfilling God's purpose for me.

God also has a purpose for you, and if you want to see if fulfilled, you need to take care of your body. No matter how you've felt in the past, decide today to take care of your temple and begin thanking God as King David did: "I will praise You, for I am fearfully and wonderfully made; marvelous are Your works, and that my soul knows very well" (Psalm 139:14).

PRAYER

Lord, thank You for the body You've given me. I pray that You would give me a love for my body because it's Your temple. Please help me to take care of it and see that it doesn't actually belong to me, it belongs to You. In Jesus' name, Amen.

WHAT IS THE HOLY SPIRIT SAYING TO ME?

FOR FURTHER STUDY
Psalms 103, 139:14; Matthew 8:17

Day 25 | *by Elizabeth Settle*
DASHBOARD LIGHTS

■●▲

Be anxious for nothing, but in everything by prayer and supplication, with thanksgiving, let your requests be made known to God; and the peace of God, which surpasses all understanding, will guard your hearts and minds through Christ Jesus. Philippians 4:6–7

Soon after telling a group of people about a personal struggle, I felt very anxious. I couldn't figure out what was going on, so I asked the Lord, "Why am I feeling this way?" I became still, and He said, "You are feeling vulnerable, not anxious." Immediately, it made sense! I told a very personal story, and I felt exposed. In response to this revelation, I asked God to protect me. Instantly, I sensed His peace descend like a guard over my heart and mind. I gave him my anxiety (a symptom of vulnerability), and He gave me His peace.

I've heard emotions compared to dashboard lights on a car: they indicate something's going on under the surface.

Have you ever been advised to *not* pay attention to your emotions? I agree that our emotions are not designed to drive us—any more than those dashboard lights should take the wheel—but they *are* designed to tell us something. Ignoring them would be like putting tape over the check engine light.

We steward emotional health by paying attention. At some point, we must stop, look under the hood, and assess the real problem. Our emotions are not lying to us. They tell us the *truth* about our beliefs, which drive us.

So, how do we "look under the hood" of our lives? Jesus isn't only *the* great physician, He is *the* great mechanic too. He is the best diagnostician of our emotional realm. He gave us those emotions!

God is an emotional being and He made us in His image. God gets angry, pleased, sad, and jealous. Because emotions are indicators of what is happening in our soul, God uses our emotions to get our attention. And we must engage Him to fix our problems by asking questions like, *Lord, what am I feeling? Why am I feeling this way? Is there a lie that I am believing that is causing this strong emotion?*

These kinds of questions, used in cooperation with Scripture, provide incredible insight. The key is to *pay attention.* If there is a warning light illuminated on the dashboard of your soul, it may be time to pull over, get quiet, and ask God what He says about what you are feeling.

He can diagnose us, and He can repair us because He is, after all, *the* great mechanic.

PRAYER

Lord, I choose to pay attention to my emotions. Will You show me what I am feeling? What beliefs are driving those emotions? I invite You to repair areas of misbelief and bring me into greater alignment with Your truth. In Jesus' name, Amen.

WHAT IS THE HOLY SPIRIT SAYING TO ME?

FOR FURTHER STUDY
Proverbs 4:23; Isaiah 61:3; Mark 2:17

26

Day 26 | *by Jimmy Evans*
THE ORDER OF LOVE

■●▲

But when the Pharisees heard that He had silenced the Sadducees, they gathered together. Then one of them, a lawyer, asked Him a question, testing Him, and saying, "Teacher, which is the great commandment in the law?" Jesus said to him, "'You shall love the Lord your God with all your heart, with all your soul, and with all your mind.' This is the first and great commandment. And the second is like it: 'You shall love your neighbor as yourself.'"
Matthew 22:34–39

The second commandment Jesus gave us was to love others as we love ourselves. But how can we love others if we don't love ourselves as God does? To understand self-love, we need to understand that love has an order. First, we love God. Secondly, we receive God's love and value and love ourselves because of who we are in Him. Thirdly, out of the love God has demonstrated to us, we love others. Healthy, functional love must follow this order. If we remove God's love or self-love, then the dynamics and boundaries change in every relationship we have.

When I met my wife, Karen, she had the lowest self-esteem of any person I have ever met. Even though she was beautiful on the outside she was broken on the inside. Not only did she *not* love herself, she thought God hated her and she couldn't be saved.

The result for Karen was constant relational and emotional turmoil. She was devastated by every gesture of others she interpreted as judgment or rejection. People—including me—violated her personal boundaries and she felt helpless to stop it or stand up to it.

Today, Karen is one of the healthiest and most confident people you will ever meet. She loves God and herself and is able to love her family and others with a grace and confidence that flows out of her intimate relationship with God. She protects her personal boundaries and can handle judgment or rejection with ease.

You might ask: *How on earth did she change from being full of self-hate and believing God hated her to how she is today?* The answer is simple and not one human can take credit for her transformation. I saw God transform my wife daily and infuse her with His love as she simply let His Word inside of her heart.

According to Hebrews 4:12, the Word of God is alive and powerful. You don't just read the Bible—it reads you. As she began to allow the Word of God to change her, her view of herself miraculously changed. Putting the order of love in place in her life was the catalyst for becoming the emotionally healthy person she is today.

Now Karen is the best steward of God's Word I have ever known. You may not think of the Bible when you think of stewardship, but it is one of the greatest treasures in our lives. To leave it gathering dust on our nightstand or bookshelf is a waste.

I encourage you to recommit to reading, studying, and meditating on God's Word. It's an incredible gift that directs, corrects, enlightens, and transforms us. Every time we read and obey it, we are being good stewards and learning how to love God, ourselves, and others better.

PRAYER

Father, I pray today that You will fill me with Your love and heal the hurts and scars in my life. I commit to loving You and receiving Your love for me. I believe that You love me and accept me, and Your throne is a throne of grace and mercy where I am welcome at all times. I want to love others with the pure, confident love that You have for me. I commit today to be a good steward of Your Word and my relationship with You. I will seek You daily and allow You to love me, change me, and fill me with Your power. In Jesus' name, Amen.

WHAT IS THE HOLY SPIRIT SAYING TO ME?

FOR FURTHER STUDY
John 4:5–26; Hebrews 4:12–13; Isaiah 55:6–11

27

Day 27 | *by Jimmy Evans*
STEWARDING A MIRACLE

■●▲

There are diversities of gifts, but the same Spirit. There are differences of ministries, but the same Lord. And there are diversities of activities, but it is the same God who works all in all. But the manifestation of the Spirit is given to each one for the profit of all: for to one is given the word of wisdom through the Spirit, to another the word of knowledge through the same Spirit, to another faith by the same Spirit, to another gifts of healings by the same Spirit, to another the working of miracles, to another prophecy, to another discerning of spirits, to another different kinds of tongues, to another the interpretation of tongues. But one and the same Spirit works all these things, distributing to each one individually as He wills. 1 Corinthians 12:4–11

When Gateway first began, we had one of our first presbytery services in which prophetic words would be given. I was one of the presbyters, and during a service the Lord told me to give a young lady in the congregation a word. And the word terrified me. He told me to tell her that she was a witch, her mother was a witch, and her grandmother was a witch and the Lord was going to deliver her that night. He told me to give her that word publicly.

I was miserable. As I sat on the platform looking at her in the congregation I silently begged God not to have to give her that word. But He didn't relent. So in the kindest manner I could, I gave her that word. She received the word with a pleasant look on her face and sat down afterward without much expression. After the service was over she approached me in the front of the auditorium, and I dreaded the encounter.

But to my surprise she walked up to me and said: "Pastor Evans, I can't tell you what your words tonight mean to me. You are right. I am a witch and have practiced witchcraft for many years. And my mother and grandmother are also witches—it has run in my family for generations. And the young man that was sitting next to me tonight is a Satanist and he came with me to see if there was any power in God."

That young lady and young man both got saved that night and were both delivered from the occult. After I heard her testimony I felt like a genius, but it had nothing to do with me at all.

Did you know, as believers, we can do miracles through the power of the Holy Spirit? The nine gifts of the Spirit the Apostle Paul tells us about in today's Scripture are not just for a special few. They are distributed to all of us if we will believe in them and receive them.

Operating in the gifts of the Holy Spirit is stewardship. Remember, being a steward means managing something that belongs to someone else. The power to do miracles is God's power. But the Holy Spirit gives that power to His people, so we can do the works of God in the lives of others. Through us, Jesus is still walking the streets, healing people, and setting them free.

I encourage you to offer yourself to the Lord to be used by Him and steward the spiritual gifts He gives you. Remember, they are gifts of grace that none of us deserve but are available to us because of the goodness and mercy of God.

PRAYER

Holy Spirit, I believe in You and the gifts You distribute to believers. I surrender myself to You and ask You to use me in whatever gift or gifts You desire. I know there are believers and unbelievers who are in need and suffering, and You want to use me to help them. I offer my mind, mouth, and body to You. Fill me with Your power and lead me with Your peace. Use me as a vessel of Your love and mercy in the lives of others. In Jesus' name, Amen.

WHAT IS THE HOLY SPIRIT SAYING TO ME?

FOR FURTHER STUDY
1 Corinthians 13–14; Luke 4:31–44

Day 28 | *by Robert Morris*
THE PRINCIPLE OF REST

■●▲

Remember the Sabbath day, to keep it holy. Exodus 20:8

I'll never forget the morning I opened my empty sock drawer and just stared at it. My mind couldn't process where all my socks had gone. Gateway Church was in its fifth year, and I had just returned from a long overseas ministry trip. The rigorous schedule of the trip capped off five years of very little rest, and as I searched for socks that weren't there, I realized how tired I was.

Have you ever been so exhausted that doing something as simple as putting on socks caused you to break down? That's what happened to me. I didn't know what to do. I was so mentally exhausted that it didn't even occur to me that I could do the laundry or buy more at Walmart. I thought, *I'm losing my mind over socks*!

Later that day, I told Pastor Tom Lane what happened, and he said, "You're not losing your mind—you're exhausted!" From that day forward, I became more diligent about stewarding my time and protecting the Sabbath day.

Isn't it funny how Christians tend to keep all of the commandments, except the one about the Sabbath? No one has a problem with the commandments that say, "You shall not commit murder" or "You shall not steal." But when it comes to the commandment about the Sabbath, so many of us think we can just ignore it. The truth is, God didn't create us for the Sabbath; He created the Sabbath for us.

It's for *our* benefit (Mark 2:27). Think of it this way. God is giving you the day off for *your good*, not for *His*.

Remember the story of the Israelites traveling through the desert? God provided manna for them to eat each day, but they were to gather only enough for that day. Then on the sixth day, God instructed them to gather enough for two days. Normally, the manna would go bad after one day, but on the seventh day—the Sabbath—it was still fresh. God wants to use the Sabbath to provide for us supernaturally, just like he did with the Israelites. God can do more for us in six days than we can do on our own in seven. We just have to trust Him. And when we do, we'll start to see blessings.

Imagine a day filled with family, delicious meals, a leisurely walk, a game of checkers, and maybe even an afternoon nap. This is a typical Jewish Shabbat (or Sabbath), but it sounds like Thanksgiving to me. The best part is, God instructed us to fit in all of our work, shopping, emails, and other obligations into six days, so we could enjoy this relaxing day *every* week, not just once a year.

This is the principle of stewarding our time and energy. So why do so many of us ignore this commandment? I believe it's because we have a difficult time trusting that God will provide for us. We think we need to work all seven days, but the Bible says God *will* provide for us if we set aside one day a week to be our Sabbath. Will you commit to trusting God and making the Sabbath a priority?

PRAYER

Lord, thank You for giving me a day off every week. Forgive me for times I haven't stewarded my rest well and help me to make rest a priority, starting with remembering the Sabbath. In Jesus' name, Amen.

WHAT IS THE HOLY SPIRIT SAYING TO ME?

FOR FURTHER STUDY
Mark 2:23–27; Exodus 20:9–10; Hebrews 4:9–11

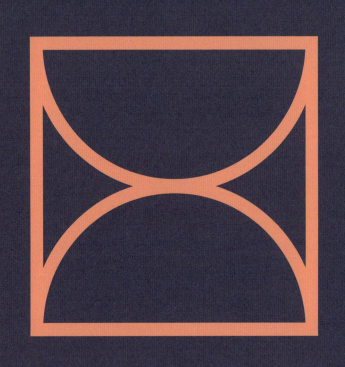